DEDICATION

To Sue, my wife and best friend.

WitWorks™
a funny little division of arizona highways books

2039 West Lewis Avenue, Phoenix, Arizona 85009.
Telephone: (602) 712-2200
Web site: www.witworksbooks.com

Publisher — Win Holden
Managing Editor — Bob Albano
Associate Editor — Evelyn Howell
Associate Editor — P. K. McMahon
Art Director — Mary Winkelman Velgos
Photography Director — Peter Ensenberger
Production Director — Cindy Mackey

Library of Congress Catalog Number: 99-62104
ISBN 1-893860-02-7

Do You Pray, Duke?
First edition published in 2001.
Printed in the United States.
Book Designer — Mary Winkelman Velgos

When I joined *Arizona Highways* in 1990, Jim Willoughby's illustrations were among the visual treasures gathered for me by the previous editor. And as I got to know Jim better, I became aware of just how talented he is: cartoonist, illustrator, sculptor, gag writer, author, historian. His cartoons have been published in many of the great magazines and one of his bronze sculptures resides in Oklahoma City's Cowboy Hall of Fame

Jim also illustrated *Arizona Highways'* first humor book, *Cow Pie Ain't No Dish You Take to the County Fair*, a book that was so successful it helped us launch a series of humor titles under the WitWorks™ imprint.

He and his wife, Sue, live in Prescott, Arizona, on the top of a hill where they feed peanuts to the birds and squirrels, and enjoy the views of the mountains and valleys around them.

Jim and Sue represent all that is good and decent in a world that is full of chaos and strife. I am proud to count them as friends.

Bob Early
Editor, *Arizona Highways*

CONTENTS

CHAPTER 1
LIFE ON THE RANGE

An aspiring cowboy singer kept telling his roundup buddies he'd like a chance to be on the stage. Finally, they put him on one.

The cowboy had a few too many before stepping out onto Dodge's main thoroughfare. His blurry eyes caught sight of Curly Bill approaching and, backed with an overabundance of liquid courage, he accosted the legendary gunman.

"Curly Bill," he challenged, "it's curtains for you!" Curly Bill's six-shooters were out of their holsters in an eyeblink and our cowboy had second thoughts.

Smiling with all the intoxicated charm he could muster, he continued, "What kind do you like?"

On a cold Wyoming winter, a shivering group of cowboys were attempting to bury a deceased comrade in a shallow grave they had managed to carve out of the icy ground. The body was stiff and longer than the grave they'd dug. One cold and impatient cowhand, stamping his nearly frozen feet on the snowcovered ground suggested, "Fold him and get him in there before he catches pneumonia!"

A real cowboy ain't too proud
to say, "I'm sorry."
Especially to a bigger guy.

SIX-PACKS AND SIX-SHOOTERS
AREN'T A GOOD MIX.

The oldtimer was on his deathbed for sure and he knew it. His ranch pals were gathered around him, listening for his final words. Looking from friendly face to friendly face, he spoke weakly, "I wish I knew if I were going to heaven or hell so I'd know which boots to take."

He learned to ride the hard way
By getting bucked around.
He spent less time in the saddle
And more time on the ground.

"WHAT'S THE BIG FUSS? FLIES ARE COMMON THIS TIME OF THE YEAR."

The elderly cowhand was understandably distressed when the doctor told him, "Your lab reports are back and they say you're dead."

"I can lick any man in the house!" the cowboy announced with that air of self-assurance that makes a cowboy a cowboy. That was moments before he found himself lying in the dust outside the swinging doors.

"Reckon," he groaned, "I was in the wrong house."

**A TORNADO IS LIKE BEIN' ON
A BUCKING BRONCO.
THEY'RE BOTH A BUMPY RIDE.**

"Buck," one cowboy observed to another, "You sure put away a lot of likker last night. How come?"

Buck looked at him bleary-eyed and replied, "I was drinking to forget and it worked. I can't remember where I left my horse."

Lefty arrived back at the ranch in his badly dented pickup. One of the hands asked him what happened. "I ran into the sheriff in town," he said, "but I understand he's going to recover."

She was pretty as a picture
As she strolled across the street.
All the cowboys gathered 'round
Thinkin',"Boy, she sure looks sweet!"

One then went up and asked her
Would she like to fool around.
She clubbed him with her parasol,
Left him lyin' on the ground.

Next time you see a lady
Looking all demure and grand,
Don't make any passes at her
If a parasol's in her hand.

"IT'S MADE OF RECYCLED HEMP."

On his deathbed and barely hanging on, the old cowpoke murmured to those about him, "I'm about to leave this world but I can't decide who to leave it to."

If you can laugh when the barn is burning, it ain't your barn.

You can't put a rope on a tornado.

**GRIZZLY BEARS
DON'T MAKE GOOD BED PARTNERS**

"I ALWAYS WANTED
TO TRY THIS SHORTCUT."

YOU KNOW IT'S GOING
TO BE A BAD DAY WHEN:

A snarling cowdog
trots around you in circles.

The ranch foreman
calls you out of bed
with a bugle.

The hangman thoughtfully asked the doomed
rustler with the rope around his neck if he had
any last requests. "Well, yes," the burly cow thief
replied, "could I floss my teeth first?"

Always give a rattlesnake
the right-of-way.

Two cowboys, hats in hand, stood over the
grave of a recently departed comrade. One spoke
to the other, "This is the longest Shorty ever went
without a drink."

**"DANG! AN' MY INSURANCE RAN OUT
JUST LAST WEEK!"**

"HOW'D IT HAPPEN?"

"THAT'S WHAT I CALL
A 'SUSPENDED SENTENCE.'"

**"IT DON'T LOOK TOO GOOD
FOR RILEY."**

"OL' SIMS DOESN'T GIVE UP EASY."

"LET ME SAY ONE LAST THING . . ."

CHAPTER 2

"THESE LEFTOVERS LOOK LIKE THEY'VE BEEN RUN OVER!"

Cowboys often say grace before eating. Head bowed, eyes closed and hands folded, one was heard to say ". . . and please, Lord, let me live through this."

At home, the wife is boss.
Out on the range, the cook is boss.
That's where the similarity ends.
Don't try to kiss the cook.

Two cowhands were wolfing down their meals of beef and beans. One looked crosswise at his grub and said, "I understand our cook studied in Paris but I'm not sure what."

Roundup cooks have a natural affinity for colorful dialogue. One had effectively blasted an errant buckeroo with a mile-long string of creative epithets when another grinning cowhand was heard to say, "Sounds like Pete just got his swearing in for the drive."

IF YOU CAN LAUGH WHEN THE CHUCK
TASTES LIKE CHALK,
THERE'S SOMETHING REALLY WRONG.
YOU NEED TO SEE A DOC.

Wiping his mouth, the visiting dude congratulated the crusty old cook, "That was mighty fine chili. What's your modus operandi?"

The cook, pulling at his bushy mustache, replied, "I never was much into opera, sonny."

Be nice to the cook — there's a chance
he might put an extra bean on your plate.

He ain't a real cowboy if he don't know
mountain oysters ain't some kind of seafood.

**RANCH COOKS TEND TO HAVE
AN EVEN DISPOSITION — ALWAYS BAD**

"LET ME KNOW IF YOU HAVE
ANY MORE COOKING SUGGESTIONS, COWBOY."

A COWBOY, BRAGGING ABOUT HIS OUTFIT'S COOK, HAD THIS TO SAY, "HIS BEANS ARE SO POWERFUL, THEY COULD PUT A MISSILE INTO SPACE."

The last thing a cowboy hears
As he rides out to rope a cow
Is, "Do a good job, cowboy,
And don't be late for chow."

Overheard around the campfire:
"One good thing about riding roundup,
we get to eat out a lot."

Asked if he had ever been married, Charlie the
cook allowed that he had. "Once," he said.
"That's why I learned how to cook."

**"WE'RE HAVING SLICED BEEF
FOR SUPPER."**

The cowhand was obviously having a difficult time eating the food on his tin plate. His face was turning all colors. The cook strolled over and said, "It's called 'chuck beef' because one bite and you chuck it."

The young cowboy asked about the nourishment value of the chuck being dished onto his plate by the nonchalant cook. "Don't ask me about nourishment, cowboy," the cook responded, "I'm just here to fill your bellies."

"HOW LONG DID YOU SAY YOU'VE
BEEN COOKIN' ROUNDUP?"

The new roundup cook was handing out papers to all the hands coming in off the range for a bite. "Here," he explained to one, "sign this form releasing me from any responsibility."

Two cowboys were shoveling down their grub when one sized up the cook's efforts. "His cooking," he said, "makes me want to take up farming."

With his cooking stick, the cook was lifting a ragged, dirty-looking sock from the large caldron of stew he was preparing. When an observant cowhand inquired about it, the cook answered, "You'll be surprised how it enhances the flavor."

Two cowboys waiting for their plate of goodies were discussing the irascible cook. One remarked, "There's a trick to good cooking and this guy is no Houdini."

"You're right," said the other. "If his cooking was a person, they'd arrest it for attempted homicide."

"I'M GETTIN' DANGED TIRED OF HEARIN'
ABOUT YOUR MAMA'S COOKING!"

"DON'T LET THE HALO FOOL YOU."

"WE DON'T DO DOGGIE BAGS, COWBOY."

CHAPTER 3

BRINGING IN THE SHEEP

The old Daleyville church had become pretty run down over the years and the one-time wooden cross atop the steeple had been replaced with a spindly TV antenna. Two passing cowboys noticed it and one remarked wryly, "Well, you know how some people worship television."

A parishioner was down on his knees between pews when the parson came by and asked if he might pray with him. "Oh, I'm not praying," the man said. "I'm looking for a dime that fell out of the collection plate."

During a pause in the sermon, a little boy's earnest plea was heard. "Please, God," he implored, "don't let the sermon be long. I've got to be at a birthday party at one o'clock."

The collection plate was extended in front of the church member and he dutifully reached into his pocket, took out a coin and dropped it in the plate. The deacon looked at it and commented, "A nickel. I presume you'd like change."

The Sunday School teacher asked Johnny to recite the first verse of Genesis for the class. "In the beginning . . . " he started to say and then paused. "That reminds me," he continued, "I'm to play in a ballgame this afternoon."

The roughneck cowhand attending a church potluck had just washed his hands and, looking around, asked, "How come there's no towel?" A church lady standing nearby answered, "Because you just washed your hands in the punch bowl."

"EVERYBODY BROUGHT POTATO SALAD."

"What's the best thing you like about Sunday School?" the teacher asked little Billy Bob.

He thought a moment and then answered brightly, "When it's over."

The volunteers showed up early in the morning, ready to paint the church. Luke, whose job it was to bring the paint, arrived with only one gallon.

"Luke," the parson admonished, "we can't paint the whole church with one gallon of paint."

"Why not?" Luke asked. "I was going to see if that barley loaves and fish thing would work with paint."

The new volunteer secretary was alert and ready to go to work. The parson came in, greeted her warmly and said "Now, Miss Meyer, take a letter."

"Sure," she shot back. "Where to?"

A CHURCH ON TOP OF A HILL IS IDEAL.
IT'S CLOSER TO GOD.

"What did you learn in Sunday School, Alice?" her mother asked after church.

"The teacher said God answers our prayers," Alice replied, "but he doesn't take phone calls."

"'HOME ON THE RANGE' DOESN'T
SEEM VERY ECCLESIASTICAL."

Two women in the third row talked annoyingly throughout the sermon. Reverend Ross took it as long as he could and then announced, "Mrs. Cook and Mrs. Crowder, I've just come up with an eleventh commandment: Thou shalt not talk while the parson is delivering his sermon."

Modern technology has finally invaded the church. Coyote Bill was riding roundup Sunday morning and used his cell phone to call the pastor to tell him he couldn't attend the service. A voice of unknown origin at the other end of the line answered, "Hello. Thank you for calling the Little White Church. If you would like to speak with Reverend Sigafoos, push one. If you would like to talk with the choir leader, push two. If you want to talk to God, bow your head and put your hands together."

The enterprising preacher on returning home from church boasted to his wife, "Attendance has shot up since we put in the snack bar."

The parson had recited the Ten Commandments as part of his fiery sermon. As people filed past him following the service, a cowboy stopped to shake his hand and commented, "Them commandments don't leave a fellow much room to have fun, parson."

"I ALWAYS HAVE THE FEELING HE'S
TALKING STRAIGHT AT ME."

One ancient cowhand told his grandkids he was there when Noah loaded his ark and swears he overheard the following:

"Can we squeeze on two more?"
"The giraffes will have to go on the top deck."
"This would be a good time to start a circus."
"Looks like it's going to rain."
"Please have your tickets ready."
"Sorry, no carry-on luggage."
"Your turn to mop the deck."
"Can anyone play the piano?"
"We're all going to sing 'Let It Pour.'"
"I've never been on a cruise before."

As the cowboy stood in front of the table jamming his face with little pieces of cracker, the reverend leaned toward him and gently admonished, "It's a holy sacrament, cowboy, not a buffet."

Shaking hands with the preacher on his way out of church, the cowhand was asked how he liked the service. "I liked it all, parson, until the choir sang 'Bringing in the Sheep.'"

HEAVEN IS A PLACE WE ALL ASPIRE TO GO. EVEN IF IT REQUIRES WEARING A GOLD HALO.

If you find yourself sitting in church alone, there's a chance you're wearing the wrong cologne.

THE COWBOY 10 COMMANDMENTS

Thou shalt not:

• Play paddleball during church service.

• Snore during the invocation.

• Scratch your behind when you are seated next to a lady.

• Spit on the floor.

• Enter the church in mid-service. Especially on your horse.

• Blow your nose in the scarf of the lady in front of you.

• Tell the preacher, "That was one devil of a sermon!"

• Pray for unimportant things. God's a busy man.

• Call a pew a peeyew.

• Look away when the collection plate is in front of you.

"ARE WE KEEPING YOU FROM ANYTHING,
BROTHER SWEENEY?"

"WE'VE REPLACED
THE OLD COLLECTION PLATES."

CHAPTER 4

SIGNS YOU'RE NOT A REAL COWBOY

A REAL COWBOY DOESN'T:

• Take his boots off in church.

• Plant tulips in a cowpath.

A REAL COWBOY DOESN'T:

• Ride an English saddle on roundup.

• Give the boss a bouquet of carnations.
Especially when he's partial to roses.

A REAL COWBOY DOESN'T:

• Try to shoe a wild stallion.

• Go fishing in a dry streambed.

**A REAL COWBOY DOESN'T
ARGUE WITH A MOTHER COW.**

A REAL COWBOY DOESN'T:

• Put ketchup on his steak.

• Read a magazine in the midst of a stampede.

A REAL COWBOY DOESN'T:

• Wear lacey underwear.

• Bet a wad on a slow runner.

A REAL COWBOY DOESN'T:

• Make a dinner out of appetizers.

• Tell the foreman how to run the ranch.

**A REAL COWBOY
DOESN'T TRY TO BE ON BOTH SIDES
OF A BARBED WIRE FENCE.**

A REAL COWBOY DOESN'T:

• Try to ride through barbed wire.

• Ride bobsleds.

A REAL COWBOY DOESN'T:

• Mount his horse on its right side.

• Take ice cream to a picnic.

A REAL COWBOY DOESN'T:

• Feed his horse rhubarb.

• Fix flats. He gets another pickup.

A REAL COWBOY DOESN'T:

• Play the slots. He likes to be a winner.

• Serenade the cows with a trombone.

**A REAL COWBOY DOESN'T WEAR PERFUME.
HOWEVER, HE FINDS IT OKAY TO
SPLASH ON A LITTLE WATER OCCASIONALLY.**

**A REAL COWBOY
DOESN'T TRY TO MILK A BULL.**

**A REAL COWBOY DOESN'T
INSULT THE BARKEEPER.**

CHAPTER 5

TALES OF REAL COWBOYS

A REAL COWBOY:

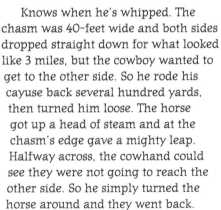

Knows when he's whipped. The chasm was 40-feet wide and both sides dropped straight down for what looked like 3 miles, but the cowboy wanted to get to the other side. So he rode his cayuse back several hundred yards, then turned him loose. The horse got up a head of steam and at the chasm's edge gave a mighty leap. Halfway across, the cowhand could see they were not going to reach the other side. So he simply turned the horse around and they went back.

A REAL COWBOY:

• Takes off his spurs before getting in his bunk.

• Knows a horse from a pickup.

A REAL COWBOY:

• Keeps his past to himself.

• Combs his hair before going courting.

A REAL COWBOY:

• Knows he's a cowboy and not a Ph.D.

• Saves room for dessert.

A REAL COWBOY:

• Tests the ice before riding out on it.

• Tips the waiter generously.

**A REAL COWBOY TAKES OFF HIS HAT
WHEN A LADY ENTERS THE ROOM.**

**A REAL COWBOY LETS THE
PREACHER DO THE TALKING.**

A REAL COWBOY DRESSES
TO SUIT THE OCCASION.
JEANS, SCUFFED BOOTS, A SCARF, A VEST AND
A WIDE-BRIMMED HAT SUIT ALL OCCASIONS.

A REAL COWBOY:

• Keeps his head when all about him are losing
theirs. That way, he'll be taller than everyone else.

• Sucks lollipops, not Marlboros.

A REAL COWBOY:

• Knows Indian smoke signals don't
bode good things.

• Cups his cards close to his chest.

A REAL COWBOY:

• Cashes in while he's ahead.

• Aims before he shoots.

A REAL COWBOY IS
ALWAYS A GENTLEMAN.

A REAL COWBOY:

• Knows a Brahma bull from a steer.

• At least pretends he likes country-Western music.

A REAL COWBOY:

• Takes a bath at least once a week.

• Knows that cowpunching goes better
when he and his horse are headed
in the same direction.

"LEMME
SEE YOUR RESUME."

A REAL COWBOY
CHOOSES HIS FRIENDS WISELY.

**A REAL COWBOY
SIPS HIS LIKKER SLOWLY.**

**A REAL COWBOY
HELPS OLD LADIES ACROSS THE
STREET . . . WELL, YOUNG ONES, TOO.**

A REAL COWBOY DARNS HIS OWN SOCKS.

**A REAL COWBOY KNOWS
A HOT IRON BRANDS MORE EFFECTIVELY.**

A REAL COWBOY TALKS NICE TO STRANGERS.
ESPECIALLY BIG ONES.

CHAPTER 6

"WHERE DOES IT HURT?"

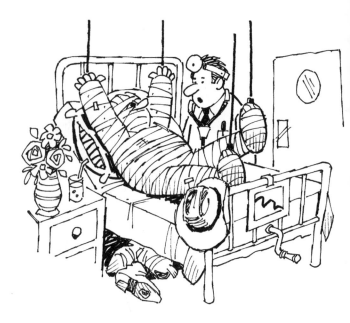

Going to the doctor beats going to the cemetery.

You might be feeling swell but if you notice a
buzzard tailing you, reassess your circumstances.

If you take away his guitar,
a cowboy becomes unstrung.

**BUCK'S THROAT WAS FEELING RAW
AND HE WENT TO THE DOCTOR TO SEE ABOUT IT.**

"FIRST THING, LET'S GET RID OF THAT ROPE."

"I'M TAKING YOU OFF THAT STEAK DIET."

The old cowboy finally had to face up to it. His bifocals were no longer getting the job done. He rode his bay mare into the town to see the optometrist and explained his problem. The doc gave him the usual tests and told the old boy, "Your tests seem okay. There's nothing wrong with your eyes. My diagnosis is that you are probably wearing your truss too tight."

ON THE OPERATING TABLE
IS A GOOD PLACE
TO TALK WITH GOD.

Good medicine usually tastes bad.

The cowboy, when asked why he had that bandage around his head, said he had been hit over the head in a barroom brawl and his doctor told him he had a "conclusion of the brain."

An old cowhand over in Wickenburg slipped a disk in his back while getting off his horse. He blamed the horse, of course, and shouted some creative profanity at it. The sensitive horse kicked him a good one. Now his jaw was broke and he was minus several teeth, but his disk jarred back in place.

"FIRST, LET'S DISCUSS
HOW SICK YOU CAN AFFORD TO BE."

Whatever you do, don't get sick on Wednesday.
That's when most doctors play golf.

When the sawbones tells you you have
acute appendicitis, he isn't flattering you.

Trust the medical man to make you better.
Still, a little prayer wouldn't hurt.

Don't call the police department
for a cardiac arrest.

BE REEEEAL NICE
TO THE NURSE WITH THE HYPODERMIC.

The aged wrangler handed a worn photograph
to a younger cowpoke and said, "This here picture
is of my wife, Gertrude. We fell in love at first
sight." Surprised, the young hand commented,
"But . . . but, Charlie, you're blind."

"Yeah," Charlie smiled wistfully, "and her
eyesight ain't none too good, neither."

Hold on there.
You don't have to remove your shirt
in an optometrist's office.

"DOCTOR HAZELTON WILL BE YOUR SURGEON.
WE CALL HIM 'OLD BUTTERFINGERS.'"

It isn't necessary to tip the anesthesiologist.

The mean old ranch foreman was just back from a stay in the local infirmary and was shouting oaths at the various wranglers like a Marine Corps drill sergeant. One of them commented to another, "They say he had a heart transplant but it still seems like he don't have one."

You don't go see a podiatrist for an upset stomach.

BE NICE TO THE UNDERTAKER.
SOONER OR LATER
HE'LL GET YOU DOWN.

Bedpans don't make good sleeping companions.

You know you're getting up in years if
you have to go to the cemetery to visit a friend.

Speaking of one of the larger cowhands, a diminutive cowboy told his pal, "He's so huge, Mail Pouch contracted with him to wear their advertising on his back. In fact, he's so big, he uses prescription window panes for eyeglasses."

"TAKE TWO OF THESE AND UPDATE YOUR WILL."

As the old-timer lay in bed, about to gasp his last earthly breath, the sweet smell of sourdough biscuits wafted over his titillated nostrils. The urge to taste one last wonderful biscuit before going to the great beyond was overwhelming.

With considerable determination, he struggled from under the covers, fell to the floor and crawled laboriously to the top of the lengthy staircase. He rolled and tumbled to the bottom, crawled with much effort to the kitchen where his wife had been busily baking a large batch of delectable biscuits and reached his faltering arm desperately up to the baking pan on the table. His knobby hand wrapped around a large, warm, yummy biscuit when — BLAM — his wife swatted him with a wet dish towel.

The biscuit dropped back in the pan and the ailing old cowpoke looked up at his stern-faced wife. "Why?" he managed. "Why did you do that?"

"Them biscuits are for the funeral," she said.

Always take something to read in the physician's waiting room. You may be there awhile. But don't show up for your appointment with a copy of the *Home Medical Advisor*.

**"I GREW THIS BEARD
SITTING IN YOUR WAITING ROOM."**

"DR. BRYERS, YOU'VE GOT TO
COME AND SEE THIS!"

"FACE IT, ROUNDUP,
YOUR SPURS AREN'T GOING TO
JINGLE JANGLE JINGLE ANYMORE."

**"MAYBE YOU SHOULD COOL IT
WITH THE SMOKING, BARNEY."**

CHAPTER 7

THE COWBOY'S ABCs

A IS FOR ACE, SECOND COUSIN TO A DEUCE.

B IS FOR BANDANA, A POPULAR TROPICAL FRUIT.

C IS FOR COLT, A YOUNG HORSE PACKING A PISTOL.

**D IS FOR DEWLAP, AS IN
"THAT KITTY SURE DO LAP UP THE MILK!"**

**E IS FOR EARMARK, A DEPRESSION LEFT IN THE PILLOW
WHEN ONE SLEEPS ON HIS SIDE.**

**F IS FOR FENCE, SOMETHING TWO GUYS
DO WITH SWORDS.**

G IS FOR GREENHORN, A COWBOY WITH GREEN HORNS.

H IS FOR HOOSEGOW, AS IN "WOW! WHO'S GAL ISSAT?"

I IS FOR IRON, WHAT A COWBOY WEARS ON HIS HIP.

J IS FOR JEANS, AS IMPORTANT TO COWBOYS AS BEANS.

**K IS FOR KETTLE,
AS IN THE SONG "KETTLE LONG, LITTLE DOGIE, KETTLE LONG."**

**L IS FOR LARIAT, AS IN
"NO I AIN'T SEEN LARRY, YET."**

**M IS FOR MAVERICK,
A COWBOY WHO TENDS TO GO THE OTHER WAY.**

N IS FOR NORTHER, OPPOSITE OF SOUTHER.

O IS FOR OUTLAW, PREFERABLE TO IN-LAW.

**P IS FOR PANHANDLE,
THE NORTHERN PART OF TEXAS.**

 **Q IS FOR QUICKDRAW,
THE FASTEST SKETCH IN THE WEST.**

 R IS FOR RAWHIDE, WHICH IS
WHAT YOU GET WHEN YOU'VE BEEN
IN THE SADDLE TOO LONG.

S IS FOR STAMPEDE,
WHICH YOU NEVER WANT TO GET IN FRONT OF.

T IS FOR TINHORN, A CHEAP MUSICAL INSTRUMENT.

 U IS FOR UNDERBRUSH, WHAT SOME COWBOYS WEAR UNDER THEIR NOSES.

**V IS FOR VOUCHER,
WHICH IS SOMEONE WHO SPEAKS WELL OF YOU.**

WHY, SURE, I'LL VOUCH FOR OLD WHAT'S 'IS NAME!

**W IS FOR WRANGLER
WHO, IF HE'S NAUGHTY,
BECOMES A DANGLER.**

**X IS FOR — FORGET X,
THERE'S NOT MUCH TO BE SAID FOR IT.**

Y IS FOR YEARN, A POPULAR FIGURE OF SPEECH.

Z IS FOR ZORRILLAS, ZORRO'S GIRLFRIEND.

"WHERE'D YOU WORK BEFORE HERE?"

Waco Wally was making a pitch to the town banker for a loan to get him and his family through the monsoon season. When they touched on the subject of collateral, the banker spoke up, "I'm really sorry, Charlie, but 'Scout's word of honor' isn't going to hack it."

Don't put your money on a three-legged nag.

When you loan money to a fellow cowhand, make sure he gives you some kind of cowlateral.

Why is it that Hollywood cowboys are so often depicted wearing big guns on their hips? Cowboys don't shoot cows, they herd them.

"HEY, SLIM, THIS KID IS LOOKING FOR
SOME DUDE NAMED DADDY WARBUCKS."

Sipping a cold brew one afternoon in the Palace Saloon, the old wrangler waxed eloquent to his fellow imbibers about his Jeep's gear ratio. One cowpoke interceded, asking how the old-timer knew all that technical jargon. "I read up on it in an encyclopediment," he replied.

Blustery Bob wasn't the kind of cowpoke you'd catch crying, but there he was standing on Main Street crying his eyes out. "Whoa, Bob, whatsa matter, kid?" a friend asked. "It's my first day off in seven weeks," Bob sobbed, "and I just found out Sully's Saloon is burnt to the ground."

A giant grizzly had Steubenville Steve up a tree and it was growing late. Glancing at his pocket watch, Steve mused, "Looks like I'm gonna be late for supper." A quizzical look crossed his face as he mused further, "Or maybe I'm gonna BE supper!"

"I'M KEEPING MY PROMISE THAT, IF ELECTED SHERIFF, I WOULD CLEAN UP TOMBSTONE."

Bobtail Billy was trying to buy some new jeans and he was being particular about it. As the salesman proudly held up a pair of his best, Billy asked, "Are they tough in the seat? I sit a lot."

Your banker has heard every reason
for someone wanting a loan.
Try just sitting there bawling.

BLACKJACK BONESTELL
WEARS A 10-GALLON HAT
ON HIS HALF-GALLON HEAD.

"THE BOYS DON'T TAKE KINDLY TO JOKES
ABOUT DECLINING CATTLE PRICES, SNODGRASS."

"THE TRICK IS GETTING BACK DOWN."

In movies, cowboys usually wear impressive six-shooters. In real life, most cowboys don't know a six-shooter from a peashooter.

Bisbee Bob entered the bunkhouse and announced to the other cowpokes present, "The boss says he has to let us all go so the ranch can stay afloat. I don't know about you guys but it's okay with me. I never could swim."

A RING OF TRUTH

Cowboys courting ladies
Should remember just one thing;
It won't be long before
They'll be hinting for a ring.

This cowboy's hat was so big, he used it for a canoe once in a heavy rainstorm.

**"KIBSEY SEES THE WORLD
THROUGH THE EYES OF AN ARTIST."**

Spring is when birds and cowboys like to nest.

The owner of the ranch was so rich,
whenever he wrote a check,
the bank had to float a loan to cover it.

The Stragnells were so rich,
the walls of their outhouse
were covered with Charlie Russell originals.

The ranch foreman was outlining his plans for
the 100,000-acre spread. He wanted to seem
democratic, however, and he told his assembled
cowboys, "I want to hear your opinions. The way
things have been going, I could use a good laugh."

His mother-in-law railed and railed at him.
Finally, he put her on a train.

You never saw a bull this big. He was so big,
he had to be shipped
to the slaughterhouse in two trucks.

You know the boss is going to let you go
when you get a note from him saying,
"It's been good knowing you."

NEVER BUY A HORSE THAT BARKS.

They say in Sonoita there's a snake under every
bush. And several in every card game.

If you're out looking for stray cows
and you hear an "Oink, Oink," keep looking.

Computers have their virtues
but you can't rope a heifer with one.

**JOHN WAYNE WAS TALL IN THE SADDLE.
JOHN WAYNE WAS TALL ANYWHERE.**

"I HATE THESE SHORTCUTS!"

CHAPTER 9

IF HORSES COULD TALK

Cowboys have a high regard for horses.

Most other people think of them in the "dumb animal" category. Dumb they ain't!

Horses have feelings like you and I.

And they have thoughts, much like you and I do.

We interviewed a few recently and they were candid in expressing their thoughts.

Here's what they had to say.

"ON ME, A PONYTAIL LOOKS OKAY."

"YOU KNOW I DON'T LIKE HORSERADISH, MILDRED!"

"HE'S A GOOD COWPUNCHER,
BUT HIS SINGING LACKS SOMETHING."

"I'M ON THE WAGON,
SO TO SPEAK."

 "LET IT RAIN, LET IT RAIN, LET IT RAIN!"

"IS THIS WHERE THE CHRISTMAS PARTY IS?"

"I WROTE TO ANN LANDERS,
BUT SHE NEVER WROTE BACK."

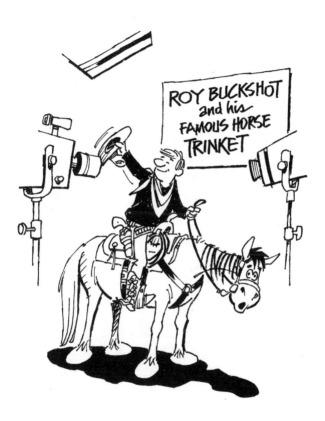

"HE GETS A MILLION DOLLARS A MOVIE,
AND I GET A BALE OF HAY."

"IF I'M ELECTED PRESIDENT,
THERE WILL BE A BALE OF HAY IN EVERY BARN."

"HAVEN'T YOU EVER SEEN A HORSE BEFORE?"

CHAPTER 10

"OTHERWISE, HOW WAS
THE TRAIL DRIVE?"

A COWBOY'S LIFE

A cowboy's life ain't easy,
He's got a lot to do.
Just chasin' cows ain't all there is;
There's jobs that make him blue.

Like mendin' fence and windmills
And even darnin' socks.
He'd rather be out bulldoggin'
Or ridin' through the rocks.

So, hats off to the cowboy,
He deserves much admiration.
He works real hard week after week
And seldom takes a vacation.

I know a cowboy who is no good without his
coffee in the morning. In fact, he's no good
with or without his coffee.

They tell of this cow that was so cantankerous,
even the cook stayed out of her way.

Seventy cowboys came to town for the annual
Cowboy Poets Gathering. Makes you wonder who's
watching the cows.

A COWBOY IS ONLY AS GOOD AS
THE HORSE HE'S RIDIN'.

On his way to the train station for a trip back home, the cowboy stepped into the local saloon for a fast one. He set his suitcase on the floor and took a stool. The barkeep served him a tall one and, looking inquisitively down at the cowboy's luggage, asked, "Gonna stay awhile?"

The carnival was in town and Slipshod Sims was entranced with the clever manipulations of Mort the Magician. As he stood there with his homely wife, Slipshod watched Mort deftly cause rabbits and doves to disappear into his high hat. A radiant glow lit his face. He leaned in close to Mort and, mentioning his wife, whispered, "How much?"

**"THAT'S NOT A 'POKER FACE.'
HE'S DEAD!"**

Theirs was a whirlwind courtship. He courted her and a whirlwind carried her away.

RODEO REALITY

We never knew a rodeo
That wasn't first or last or best;
They wear out all the adjectives;
Let's put this thing to rest.

There are horses, cows and cowboys
Getting busted up for sure;
Why the heck those cowboys do it
Is just so much manure.

They limp around and brag
How long they stayed aboard.
Or, sipping on a brew, they tell
How often they've been gored.

Still, folks go to see the rodeo,
First or last or best.
With all its twists and bucks and bumps,
It's the sport that won the West.

Discussing the desperate local job situation, one cowhand said he wasn't worried about losing his. "There ain't no way they can round up cows with a computer," he explained.

"THIS LOOKS LIKE A GOOD PLACE."

The airline stewardess asked the travelling cowboy if he had anything to put in the overhead compartment. The cowboy pointed to his outsized Resistol and replied, "Ma'am, my hat is all the overhead luggage I've got."

A POETIC THOUGHT

These cowboy poets would be better off
And so would the ranches they ride for
If, instead of writin' poetry,
They'd work a little more.

Two cowboys were browsing through the town's only drugstore. One idly lifted a medicine bottle from its shelf and observed. "Boy, they've got cures for sicknesses that ain't been invented yet."

"YOU'VE GOT TO GET
A TALLER HORSE, RHUBARB."

"I DON'T THINK YOU'VE QUITE GOTTEN
THE HANG OF BUILDING FENCE, HENDERSON."

The stewardess laboriously made her way down the airplane's aisle, trying to comfort the shaken-up passengers, assuring them that the turbulence would soon subside. A grizzled wrangler tipped his tall hat to her and said, "Ma'am, I've been bucked around a lot more'n this ol' airplane could ever manage."

A gent running for political office came stumping through the central Arizona ranch lands. Visiting the K4 Ranch in northern Yavapai County, he betrayed his lack of knowledge concerning grazing matters by waving his finger in the air and declaring, "If I am elected to the State Senate, I'll see to it that there is a cow in every garage – er – is it a barn?"

One old cowboy said that when he was a kid his family was so poor he had to eat scraps left over by the hogs.

A cowboy on the Lazy-U couldn't get a horse to stay under him. It isn't to say he didn't ride well but every time he'd start to mount up, the horse would break up laughing.

"AFTER YOU'RE HERE ON THE DESERT AWHILE,
CACTUS JUST KIND OF GROWS ON YOU."

This wrangler, wanting to better himself, took a night course in arithmetic. When one of his buddies asked him how much was one and one, he replied, "We ain't got that far yet."

"I ain't sayin' he's expensive," a cowhand related to his bunkmates, "but after examining me this doctor called up his wife and told her to go out and get that mink coat she'd been wanting."

To the question, "Why did you become a cowboy?" the new hand responded, "I wanted to be a butcher but I didn't have the guts."

Saddling his horse one frosty morning, an old cowboy told his partner, "I watched TV last night and they used language you wouldn't hear in the ranch house."

Beside a sign clearly indicating "VALET PARKING," a cowhand atop his pony explained to the parking attendant, "I don't want to park a valet. I want to park my horse."

A rugged looking cowboy was telling his pals his family had been so poor when he was a kid, he had to wear his sister's hand-me-downs.

A proud cowhand was showing off his brand new winter coat to his bunkmates. One of them commented, "The boss ain't going to like you wearin' a sheepskin jacket, Maynard."

"WELL, YOU SURE UNSTUCK IT!"

"OLD IKE SURE CAN MAKE A LARIAT TALK."

"OF COURSE, YOU NEED A STEPLADDER TO GET MOUNTED."

"IT'S A LITTLE TIGHT AROUND THE NECK."

"WHEN THE RANCH BECOMES
A GOLF COURSE, I WANT TO BE READY."

"YEP, IT'S BEEN A BUSY DAY."

"WEREN'T YOU BIG STUFF
IN ARABIA ONCE, LARRY?"

"OL' GEORGE SITS TALL IN THE SADDLE, THOUGH."

"ACTUALLY, IT LOOKS BETTER IN 'ARIZONA HIGHWAYS.'"